D0240778

Dealing with
Bullying at Work

in a week

RUTH WHEATLEY

Hodder & Stoughton

A MEMBER OF THE HODDER HEADLINE GROUP

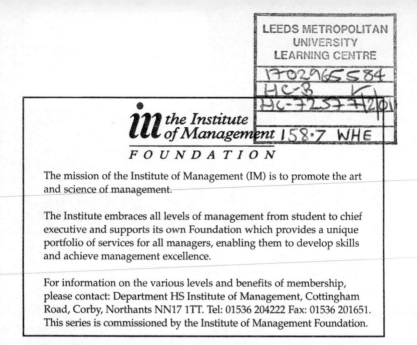

**the Institute
of Management**

F O U N D A T I O N

The mission of the Institute of Management (IM) is to promote the art and science of management.

The Institute embraces all levels of management from student to chief executive and supports its own Foundation which provides a unique portfolio of services for all managers, enabling them to develop skills and achieve management excellence.

For information on the various levels and benefits of membership, please contact: Department HS Institute of Management, Cottingham Road, Corby, Northants NN17 1TT. Tel: 01536 204222 Fax: 01536 201651. This series is commissioned by the Institute of Management Foundation.

Orders: please contact Bookpoint Ltd, 78 Milton Park, Abingdon, Oxon OX14 4TD. Telephone: (44) 01235 827720, Fax: (44) 01235 400454. Lines are open from 9.00 - 6.00, Monday to Saturday, with a 24 hour message answering service. Email address: orders@bookpoint.co.uk

British Library Cataloguing in Publication Data
A catalogue record for this title is available from The British Library

ISBN 0 340 74751X

First published 1999
Impression number   10 9 8 7 6 5 4 3 2 1
Year   2005 2004 2003 2002 2001 2000 1999

Copyright © 1999 Ruth Wheatley

Cover photo from TCL Stock Directory.
Typeset by Multiplex Techniques Ltd, St Mary Cray, Kent.
Printed in Great Britain for Hodder & Stoughton Educational, a division of Hodder Headline Plc, 338 Euston Road, London NW1 3BH by Cox & Wyman Ltd, Reading, Berkshire.

C O N T E N T S

INTRODUCTION

Bullying at work can destroy people and undermine organisational performance. Research shows it to be a growing problem in the UK, and one which tends to go unreported in many cases.

The unhappiness caused by bullying (sometimes for the perpetrators as well as for the bullied) inevitably undermines morale and working relationships. For individuals who are bullied at work, the effects can be crippling, and there are now increasing numbers of documented cases that have resulted in illness and breakdowns. For organisations, the effects may be equally damaging, in the form of sickness absence, high stress levels, lowered performance and poor morale.

In the UK there is no legislation specific to workplace bullying at present, but employers can be vulnerable to expensive cases related to bullying.

Discouraging workplace bullying involves:

- being clear about what bullying is and the damage it can do
- knowing how to respond to bullying
- identifying bullies
- providing support for those who are involved in bullying
- setting up preventative strategies

The words of some of the people whose words have informed this text may help to illustrate the sort of suffering that workplace bullying can inflict:

The effect of the bullying on me was extreme: the stress, absolute misery and fear contributed to illness which resulted in my being signed off work for four months.

Manager.

4

■ I N T R O D U C T I O N ■

*I was punished, and am still being punished, for pursuing
my case.*

Health service worker.

*During the year that I worked for her I suffered from IBS,
related to stress, panic attacks and nervous exhaustion. I
lodged a complaint, but it has been dismissed.*

College administrator.

*I know that many people still dismiss the severity of
bullying – probably this time last year I, too, would have
said it was something which could only happen to weak
characters or 'losers', but having been a victim of it I know
that it really can happen to anyone.*

Professional worker.

Over the next week, we will seek answers to the following
questions:

- what is a bully?
- who are the workplace bullies?
- are you being bullied?

We will then learn about:

- support for those bullied at work
- controlling bullying in the organisation
- bullying and management

On Saturday, we will recap our progress during the week,
and draw some final conclusions about how bullying can
be dealt with and prevented.

So what is a bully?

Today, we will focus on what bullying is and the sort of behaviours that are involved. We will consider:

- the meaning of workplace bullying
- different levels and types of workplace bullying
- the growth of the problem of bullying at work

Bullied people will be referred to throughout as either recipients or complainants, depending on the context. This is because many people who experience workplace bullying prefer not to be labelled as victims.

We are all able to make choices, and to challenge the wrong behaviour of bullies, but it should always be remembered that people who are being bullied will find the situation very hard to deal with. Challenging a bully is tough, and only those who have never experienced workplace bullying are likely to think that taking action about it is easy.

BULLY   CHALLENGER

What does bullying mean?

A bully can be defined as a person who hurts, persecutes or intimidates others, though as we will see later, the word 'bullying' is emotive and means different things to different people.

A definition of bullying as 'persistent intimidation which humiliates and demoralises another person or other people' will be our working definition for this week. It will be qualified by the recognition that bullying is not always conscious and deliberate, and can result from poor management in organisations or bad behaviour by individuals.

Workplace bullying may occur in private, or it may be very public. It is based on the abuse of power, and the power is most often derived from seniority. It could also, though, be derived from:

- physical threat
- psychological domination
- the pressure of a group

Bullying behaviour can be directed at a single individual or at a group of individuals. In the UK, recipients have generally been viewed as most likely to be lone individuals, though a UNISON research project reported in 1998 suggested that more people are actually bullied in groups.

Sometimes we may all feel the impulse to consciously bully others. But most of us learn to restrain that impulse, just as we learn to restrain other damaging or illegal impulses.

Bullying becomes serious and pathological when it is regular and inescapable.

Workplace bullying

Bullying at work is particularly insidious because:

- it can hold the recipient's livelihood to ransom
- it is usually carried out by someone who holds a position of trust and authority
- for as long as it continues unchecked, it is implicitly condoned by the employing organisation

The toleration of, or failure to prevent, bullying in the workplace is irresponsible management, because bullying damages all those involved, especially the organisation itself.

Physical violence

Physical assault or violence is not necessarily a symptom of bullying, if it is a one-off outburst. Where violence is persistent, however, it is the most obvious form that bullying can take, and is not as hard to prove as other types of bullying.

Dealing with violence in disciplinary terms can be difficult if no witnesses are present, but most organisations have policies in place to deal with this sort of physical behaviour.

Being prepared for violence at work

- Never use violence unless forced to: most organisations view any fighting as gross misconduct, whatever the circumstances
- Learn about elementary forms of self-defence in case you are forced to defend yourself
- Be aware of the usual reaction to violence of paralysed inaction: mentally rehearse how you could respond to violence at work

- Do not let yourself be cornered by the potential attacker
- Keep your front and face turned towards him or her
- Appear calm, but not arrogantly so
- Get the attention of the potential attacker and establish communication
- Try diversionary tactics
- Talk to try to redirect the attacker's attention
- Look for escape routes
- If escape is possible, move slowly, keeping your face to the potential attacker and trying to make sure obstacles are placed between the attacker and yourself.

Most bullying at work is not blatant physical violence but psychological violence, though bullying at work in all its forms seems to be a growing problem. We will focus upon both unconscious and deliberate psychological bullying over this week.

Store rage

Violence in stores, or 'store rage', was reported as running at 350,000 incidents of customer aggression towards store workers in 1995. Levels of abuse and threats were also found to be increasing.

Causes identified included long check-out queues, attempted theft and anger about poor service or low quality.

Source: Independent on Sunday,
22 September 1996, p. 10.

* *Unconscious bullying*

Bullying can be unintended behaviour on the part of a bully who is unaware of the full effects of his or her behaviour. It may even remain unrecognised by bullied people, in that they may not accept the reality of bullying as the source of their low morale and general unhappiness.

The person who bullies unconsciously may be aware of causing others offence but view the behaviour as being simply:

* strong management
* direct and 'to the point' communication
* close supervision to improve productivity management

Deliberate bullying

Deliberate bullying occurs when someone persistently and knowingly seeks to harass and hound selected individuals while disguising this behaviour from others. Such bullying can be very difficult to prove and to deal with. Cases of deliberate bullying often centre on an individual who seems to most people to be charming and incapable of deliberately bad behaviour. As a result, the complaints of those who are bullied in such circumstances are often disbelieved. The deliberate bully's behaviour can be related to various factors, including:

- personality type and psychology
- organisational culture and management style
- job role insecurity

Types of bullies

Charlotte Rayner of Staffordshire University has identified various types of bullies, including people who:

- explode angrily, in either an indiscriminate or a focused way
- target those they dislike or consider poor performers
- bully those they consider to be a threat to their own position
- are bullied themselves and 'pass the parcel'
- think deliberate bullying is the best way to make people work harder
- bully after 'being nice' fails to get the required results
- bully sadistically, for their own pleasure
- want to push staff into resigning
- bully to give themselves a 'macho' image

Source: Daily Telegraph, 8 March 1996, p. 5.

Behaviours that are bullying

Bullying at work is evidenced in many ways and by many behaviours. It might, for example, be:

Either:	Or:
• deliberate and planned	• random and unconscious
• explicit and obvious	• hidden and secret
• rooted in individual psychology	• encouraged by organisational culture

If all possible forms of bullying behaviour were to be listed, they would take up several pages of this book. Some obvious examples include:

- actual or threatened violence
- frequent and loud criticism
- shouting and verbal assault
- sarcasm
- ostracising or 'sending to Coventry'
- public smear campaigns

Most often, bullying is a subtle, hidden and repetitive process, typified by small events and persistent, petty harassment. It makes an impact through the gradual build-up of the effects of daily repetition, which slowly break down a recipient's confidence and morale.

E-mail bullying or 'flamemail'

A study of bullying by e-mail (known as 'flamemailing') found that the most common reaction of people who were flamemailed was to send a flamemail back in reply.

Source: Shaming, Blaming and Flaming: Corporate Miscommunication in the Digital Age, *London, Firefly Communications, 1996.*

A bully will usually combine various behaviours or tactics. To those hearing a bullying complaint, the incidents described may seem petty. But if they are persistent and frequent over a sustained period, these petty incidents will be extremely destructive in their effects.

Examples of bullying tactics

Constant criticism	Giving too much work
Ridicule	Giving too little work
Belittling achievements	Giving responsibility without authority
Stealing credit for achievements	Refusing leave
Stealing ideas	Marginalising
Making false accusations	Fault finding
Setting obviously unrealistic targets	Blocking promotion

The growing problem of workplace bullying

Reports of bullying at work are increasing, though the higher rate of complaints is sometimes linked to factors such as greater awareness of the problem of workplace bullying or more awareness of individual rights.

Facts and figures
- 1994 IPD survey: one in eight UK employees said they had been bullied within the previous five years
- 1995 Staffordshire University research:
  - half of those asked had experienced workplace bullying
  - 78 per cent had seen colleagues being bullied
- 1998 TUC survey: this estimated that up to five million people could be bullied at work in the UK

- 1998 Andrea Adams Trust research: nearly half of those asked had experienced workplace bullying; eighty per cent said that they knew of a bully in their workplace
- 1999 IRS survey: over the last two years 15% of employers have been confronted with a tribunal case related to bullying

Statistics are always arguable, especially when they refer to a subjective concept such as bullying. But there is no doubt of the workplace misery caused by bullying that has been uncovered by various research projects, and by initiatives such as the TUC's Bullying Hotline, which was contacted by thousands of people. The extent of the problem has consistently been shown as far greater than was previously thought.

Increased awareness of bullying at work

During the early and mid-1990s, publicised documentaries about real experiences of workplace bullying heightened general levels of awareness of the subject for a wide, public audience. The pioneering work of Andrea Adams for the BBC on workplace bullying was particularly important in bringing the subject to the attention of the general public.

Sometimes, it is argued that increased awareness of workplace bullying as an issue may itself cause more complaints to be made. There is an element of truth in this, and some bullying complaints may be spurious or refer to justified behaviour or activities that are not actually bullying.

Research suggests, however, that most people who are bullied at work suffer for long periods before becoming desperate enough to complain, and often refuse to complain despite prolonged bullying. Reported cases, therefore, may actually under-represent the full extent of cases of workplace bullying.

The 'no-win' situation for bullied people

Too many employers still prefer not to recognise cases of bullying, even when it is blatant and causing:

- distress to the recipient
- obvious problems or losses for the organisation

For this reason, taking action against bullying is difficult. When the experience of bullying becomes destructive enough to make action a necessity, people have to choose between leaving their employing organisation, or openly challenging the bullying situation.

At the same time that the recipient has to make this hard choice, he or she will usually be severely demoralised and possibly physically ill as a result of the bullying.

Even if recipients go all the way in challenging workplace bullying, and have the satisfaction of winning their case and gaining compensation, they often still feel that they have lost out in the end. They cannot replace the job they may have lost, or easily repair the long-term effects of bullying in terms of:

- lost confidence
- weakened health
- continued nightmares and disturbed sleep

Summary

Today, we have defined the meaning, and considered different levels and types, of workplace bullying, and seen how it is a growing problem.

Tomorrow, we will look more closely at the costs and effects of workplace bullying, and go on to think about:

- who the bullies might be
- the subjective nature of the bullying concept

Who are the workplace bullies?

After identifying the main costs and effects of workplace
bullying, we will consider:

- characteristics of bullies and bullying behaviour
- possible sources of workplace bullying
- whether our own work behaviour is ever bullying
- the ambiguous nature of the concept of bullying
- the role of perception in the experience of bullying

Costs and effects

The costs of not caring

There are examples of six-figure penalties being
awarded in bullying cases based on harassment.

One estimate of the overall cost of lost working time

and legal fees caused by workplace bullying in the UK places it at £4 billion a year.

Source: Prof. C Cooper, Times Educational Supplement, *10 May 1996.*

Workplace bullying is difficult to deal with, but the need for action is increasingly accepted because of its severe effects on people and organisations. There are now many known cases of physical health problems, breakdowns and changes of personality that have resulted from bullying at work. Outcomes can include:

- high stress
- illness
- mental health problems
- poor performance
- demotivation
- breakdown
- suicide

An individual recipient's financial situation and career is usually badly affected, while his or her personal life and family can be devastated.

Within organisations, bullying is a problem with high costs in terms of:

- reduced efficiency and productivity
- lowered motivation and morale
- high recruitment and retraining costs
- potential legal costs and penalties
- lost working time through sickness absence

An obvious harmful effect for organisations is the risk of tribunal cases, civil actions or law suits related to bullying, and some cases have already led to high penalties for employers.

Some characteristics of bullies at work

Workplace bullies are not always the sort of people we may imagine them to be. When we hear of bullying, we tend to picture a culprit such as a rude and bossy manager, an overambitious, competitive colleague or an overzealous supervisor. But bullying at work has many causes, and takes the form of many behaviours. There is no stereotypical bully, and bullying cannot be pinned down to a particular personality type or to fixed ways of behaving. Each case of bullying is likely to be different, and takes place within a complex web formed by the personalities, psychology, organisational setting and wider context involved.

Nevertheless, some common behavioural characteristics emerge from many cases of deliberate workplace bullying:

- *Insecurity:* it is often said that the greatest bullies are also the greatest cowards. The psychology of workplace bullying is based on insecurity, and the typical bullying boss may be an inadequate manager, secretly afraid of the ability and competence of others. Bullying can be used to hide inadequacies, while the bully projects his or her own faults onto the recipient or a group of recipients.
- *'Jekyll and Hyde' character:* bullies often seem to be Jekyll and Hyde characters, appearing to be charming at one moment but behaving like tyrants the next. This sometimes makes it hard for recipients to convince those

to whom they complain that the bully is capable of bad behaviour.

- *Oversupervision or control:* the workplace bully often has an extreme need to be in control, and displays this through closely supervising every little matter, looking over people's shoulders constantly and making unnecessary shows of authority.
- *Dislike of being shown to be wrong:* the bully is often an individual who cannot bear to be proved wrong about anything, and who may try to exact revenge when this happens.
- *Dishonesty:* bullies are frequently deceitful characters who will lie to disguise their behaviour or to mislead and misinform the recipient.

Identifying workplace bullies

Case study: upward bullying

A newly-appointed manager in a care centre for elderly people was critical of the quality of care her staff were providing for clients, and sought to improve it. She found that, as a result of her efforts to improve standards of care, she was for three years bullied by the staff of five who reported to her. They sought to obstruct her, and grouped together to oppose her where possible, humiliate her verbally and tie up her time with pointless complaints. At the end of the three years, she was a nervous wreck, suffered high blood pressure, and had lost her confidence in dealing with employees. Her complaints were poorly dealt with, and she eventually resolved the situation herself by employing a supportive undermanager, using detailed risk assessments, splitting the five people whenever possible during their breaks, and replacing those who left with people who were better in their care role.

Most bullying does, in practice, seem to be by managers, supervisors and bosses, and UNISON's 1998 research corroborates other findings in identifying the most likely attribute of the bully to be his or her managerial role (83 per cent).

Case study: women can bully too

Women, when they have the power, are as likely to bully as men, and may bully men as well other women.

A bank clerk was awarded almost £5,000 on grounds of sex discrimination after being bullied by a young, female manager. The manager humiliated him by:

- insisting that he mop the floor
- regularly patronising and speaking rudely to him
- constantly watching him in a critical way

The Chairman of the Employment Tribunal inferred that the woman saw the assertive, young man as some sort of threat to her authority.

Source: The Guardian, 2 *September 1998*, p. 4.

But bullies can be any kind of person, from any working level and any professional group. They might be:

- *colleagues*, either singly or as a group, picking out an individual and harrying him or her solely with imagined justification, and with no authority;
- *customers*, especially in sectors where front-line staff have to deal with angry, complaining or violent customers. Customers may also try to use their purchasing power or their complaining influence as a means of bullying. But a one-off instance of

unpleasantness with a customer, however severe, cannot be considered as bullying. It is only when regular customers repeatedly cause problems for particular employees that they join the ranks of workplace bullies;

Case study: customer bullying

At a fish and chip shop in North London, staff were abused and harassed for over 18 months by a man who was angry after being told to take his turn in the queue. His harassment included obscene gestures, spitting and telling customers not to use the shop. The shop had to take their case to court to stop the harassment.

Source: Independent on Sunday, *22 September 1996, p. 10.*

- *reportees*, either as a group or as individuals acting alone. Upward bullying is especially likely to occur when someone appointed to supervision is resented for some reason by reportees, or tries to change things more than they wish;
- *managers*. The highest percentage of bullying reports involve managers, and for that reason the setting of appropriate management styles and standards within an organisation is an extremely important part of combating bullying behaviour at work.
- *bosses* can be guilty of bullying behaviour, and where this occurs it is very destructive for the business. Where the top person is known as a bully, either implicitly through his or her behaviour or explicitly through undisguised dominance, permission is effectively given for a bullying

management style to filter down throughout the organisation.
- *corporate attitudes* within an organisation can be bullying, possibly because standards of management are low or because conflicts arise. This may apply particularly, for example:
  - in instances of whistleblowing opposed by the organisation (although there is now strong legal protection for many whistleblowers in Britain)
  - where new hours or conditions are required
  - where a restructuring is taking place.

The human nature of bullying

It is clear that bullying personalities are not always highly visible. Bullying can be carried out by any individual or group of people. In fact, we are all likely to behave in a bullying way at times, and in some circumstances. It is a very human impulse, though not a very attractive one, and displays of bullying can occur wherever people interact in some way: in the home, in the street, during leisure activities, at school and at work.

Bullying involves aggressive behaviours of which we will all be guilty at times, and we should therefore:

- monitor our own behaviour at work for possible bullying tendencies
- seek regular feedback from those around us to help develop our understanding of how others perceive us

Are you a bully?

Everyone is likely to bully others on occasion, without necessarily being aware of the nature or the impact of their behaviour. Do you ever, for instance:

- give people tasks they cannot achieve?
- refuse requests for leave or training without good reason?
- victimise a colleague with persistent sarcasm, teasing or practical jokes that upset him or her?
- encourage unfounded or malicious gossip?
- pick out small faults, while recognising no positive value in work done?
- criticise people repeatedly, especially in front of others?

- exclude people who should be present from meetings?
- fail to give people information they should have?
- shout at people?
- change guidelines or procedures without consultation?
- treat one person very differently to others?
- ridicule the arguments of others in meetings?
- keep changing the work instructions you give to others?
- accept credit for the work or ideas of others?
- leave all instructions in note form, or pass them on through an intermediary?
- use foul or abusive language?

This list could be endless, and most of the above behaviours will only become bullying if they are repeated regularly and are carried out with aggressive intent.

Bullying as perception – the ambiguity of the bullying problem

Ambiguity is a big problem for an individual who experiences bullying, or for an organisation which attempts to manage or control bullying incidents. It is sometimes hard to agree on what constitutes bullying and, except in the most obvious or clearly witnessed cases, it can be hard to establish the truth about what has happened.

Bullying is a subjective issue, and there are no general, agreed standards by which to be sure whether bullying has occurred. Sometimes, people complain about being bullied when others might consider that the circumstances make a complaint unjustified. Equally, people who are accused of bullying may sometimes genuinely fail to agree that they are guilty of bullying.

Psychologist Charlotte Rayner has pointed out that most research is, of necessity, based on subjective, anecdotal experiences and perceptions. Furthermore, as the experience of bullying can in itself change some recipients' attitudes and ways of perceiving behaviour, it becomes doubly difficult to be sure of clear, objective research evidence on the issue.

Most people meet with situations that are ambiguous enough to seem to border on bullying at some point during their working lives. All employees are likely to experience occasional behaviours from bosses, colleagues or reportees that cause a degree of hurt, humiliation or anger, such as:

- heavy-handed wielding of authority
- unfairness
- rudeness
- malice

Even if the experience is extreme, however, it is not likely to qualify as workplace bullying, taken alone.

Mistaken complaints of bullying

Some individuals mistakenly think they are being bullied because, for example, they:

- identify justifiable and reasonable disciplinary or
  performance discussions as bullying
- fail to recognise faults in their own behaviour or attitude
  which are contributing to disagreements or conflicts
- have personal problems of a physical or psychological
  nature which cause difficulties that are related to
  communications rather than bullying

Individuals can sometimes be the unrealising cause of their
own isolation or conflicts with others, and colleagues may
find it hard to always respond with warmth to a person
who, for example, consistently:

- uses clumsy, aggressive body language
- is cold, detached and without personal interest in others
- sulks over small issues or disagreements
- has a low level of personal hygiene
- is a poor team performer
- chats too much and too often
- has unpredictable mood swings
- frequently criticises and provokes others

Individuals with characteristics like the above of which
they are unaware may come to experience and complain of
rejection, criticism or outright hostility from colleagues or
managers. But those same colleagues or managers may
well perceive the complaining individual to be bullying,
and could defend their own behaviour within the
circumstances, provided no outright malice or harassment
is involved.

This sort of situation can easily develop in employment
contexts without good communications practices, where
there is no one-to-one discussion of confidential or sensitive
matters. A perception rather than an actual case of bullying
is at issue at this stage, and needs to be detected, then
tested against reality by a mediator with sensitivity,
compassion and good interpersonal skills.

Summary

Today we have considered the main costs and effects of
workplace bullying, its characteristics and possible sources,
whether we ourselves are liable to this behaviour, and its
subjective and sometimes ambiguous nature.

Tomorrow, we will look more closely at where resolvable
problem behaviours end and bullying begins. We will then
start to consider how to deal with actual rather than
mistaken bullying at work.

Are you being bullied?

Today, we will look at dealing with difficult, critical or confrontational behaviours before they develop into a full-scale bullying problem. We will learn how to:

- use discussion and conciliation to distinguish normal behaviour problems from bullying
- handle conflicts and deal with criticisms in an adult way
- forestall much potential bullying

We will then summarise the possible response options for people who are bullied at work.

The stresses and strains of normal work

We all have pressures at work, and may have to:

- meet production or service targets
- meet deadlines
- do more than seems possible with the resources available
- deal with difficult or complaining customers
- perform well whatever the circumstances

Such pressures are an increasing factor of working life, and can affect behaviour. Within a busy, working context, and an environment of growing job insecurity, it is inevitable that more individuals are suffering stress. As a result, they sometimes panic, lose their tempers or make mistakes.

Even within a relaxed working context, team or line working relationships will involve some ups and downs, disagreements and personality clashes. At times, we all experience:

- confrontation
- criticism
- conflict
- personal rejection
- difference of opinion

Such experiences do not involve bullying in themselves, and can be met and dealt with through assertive communication skills and honesty.

What to do when you are criticised

- Consider whether the criticism was constructive and aimed to help you in some way – possibly to improve your performance or avoid a future problem.
- If you decide that the criticism was constructive, consider whether the comments were valid, and discuss them with the critic.
- If you decide that the criticism was not true, tell the critic what you think and discuss the comments further.
- Remember that invalid, destructive criticisms are based on opinion rather than fact, make no suggestions to support change, or are personally derogatory.

Bullying and job roles

Sometimes, the very nature of a particular line of work can make it seem like bullying to others while the accused themselves may consider that they were just doing their work honestly and thoroughly. This applies especially to jobs involving close inspection of the work or workplace conditions of others, such as:

- health and safety inspections
- auditing
- quality inspections

Case study: the School Inspector

A senior School Inspector was sacked following a school inspection which allegedly left many staff in tears. The complaint of bullying and intimidation made by the school was the last of a series of complaints made over three years, and led to a review of the conduct of 40 other such Inspectors.

The Inspector defended his behaviour, asserting that he had only:

- worked with efficiency and thoroughness
- communicated bluntly
- reported his findings with honesty

In the Inspector's view, the real bullying came from the pressures put on Inspectors to change their judgements.

But those who experienced the Inspector's aggressive approach were distressed to an unacceptable degree.

Source: The Guardian (Education Supplement)
8 December 1998, pp.2–3.

Your right to be treated with respect

If you are an employee, there is no magic key to dealing with bullying at work. It is a difficult area because your position is vulnerable, in that you are very much in the power of your employers. But you can decide for yourself the degree to which you accept uncomfortable or unpleasant behaviour at work. It is really a matter for individual judgement, taking into account:

- the context
- the pressures involved

- your personal knowledge of the offending person
- your experience of the organisation you work for

You have a right to be treated with respect, and should be able to assert that right in any fair and open working environment without being penalised. At the same time, to be realistic, you cannot expect absolute perfection, either in individuals or from organisations.

And, if you are honest with yourself, you are likely to find that your own behaviour towards others may sometimes be perceived as far from perfect.

Before interpreting bad behaviour as full-scale bullying, you therefore need to balance the context and factors that are relevant, then make a personal judgement on whether to challenge or tolerate the behaviour.

Being assertive about your rights
- Think carefully and objectively about the event and its context
- Clarify your feelings and the reasons for them in your own mind
- Ask the person or persons concerned if you can talk together privately
- State your feelings directly to the individual or group of individuals
- Explain your reasons with calmness, honesty and directness
- Speak plainly, but not with aggression

Do not:	Do:
• shout	• state what you feel clearly and firmly
• display anger	• state your reasons calmly
• become emotional	• remain calm if the response is loud or abusive

IT'S TIME TO HAVE THAT CHAT ...

Conciliation

If discussion is resisted, or if it is taken up and still results in disagreement, seek to bring in an adjudicator who can give a balanced outside view of the situation. This might be a colleague, a personnel official or someone with sufficient line responsibility to arbitrate and make a judgement on behalf of the organisation.

Confrontation and complaint
At any stage, the person whose behaviour you question
may react with defensive aggression and:

- angrily deny that your feelings are valid
- become upset or tearful because you are felt to be
  making a challenge
- shout abuse
- threaten disciplinary action

If you are confronted at this stage with these or similar
emotional responses, you could be dealing with a difficult
person. In a 'worst scenario' situation, he or she could be a
potential bully, so your responses will now become crucial.

Taking matters forward in such a heated context will
usually necessitate a complaint that will go on the record,
with probable immediate intervention or arbitration at an
official level.

You can decide that you are not willing to move on into
this situation. If so, your firm reaction to this particular
instance of problem behaviour may have been enough to
prevent it from recurring.

Handling conflict
Don't let yourself get stressed by the words or behaviour of
the other person or people concerned. The 'natural' reaction
to hostility, provocation or aggression might be
counterattack as a first defence, but this natural cycle only
serves to escalate conflict. Break it by:

- reacting calmly and reasonably, while remaining
  assertive
- repeating your points quietly and insistently
- knowing your facts and dealing in them as much as
  possible

Facing up to bullying

If you are certain that bullying behaviour is the main factor in your situation, and that normal communications and discussions cannot resolve your problems with a person or group of people, then you have moved into the arena of dealing with bullying at work.

From this point, be sure to keep a log of bullying incidents if you are not already doing so, and keep all documentation (such as relevant memos, appraisal forms or reports) that could support you in a tribunal hearing.

Being bullied at work - action checklist

1 Seek proof of the bullying from the moment you identify it.
2 Find out whether your employer has a policy on bullying or harassment.
3 Log every incident, recording times, dates and witnesses present.
4 Explore the possibilities of witness support.
5 Keep all relevant documentation such as memos.
6 Consider secretly recording evidence, if you have support for this from a personnel officer or higher company manager. Note that, without such support, your duty of trust and confidence to your employer could come into question.
7 Consider seeing a solicitor and making a sworn witness statement (affidavit), especially if you are sure that your organisation will not listen to your complaint.

Remember that bullying can only flourish through secrecy, and that the bully depends upon your taking no action against him or her. The first step you should take is to make a decision on which of the limited, available options you should choose to deal with the bullying:

- confront the bully directly
- make an informal complaint
- make an official complaint
- ignore the bullying
- find another job
- resign at once
- take legal action

Confront the bully directly
Talk to the bully or bullies yourself about how you feel, or get someone to do so for you. Ask him, her or them to stop bullying you. This can be an effective way to end bullying, especially if it is not deliberate.

Make an informal complaint
Talk to your boss about the bullying you are experiencing. If your boss is the bully, talk to the next manager up the line or a personnel official. He or she may be able to help you to resolve the situation without making a formal complaint.

Poor responses to complaints about workplace bullying

There are cases in which a bullied complainant has been made to feel that he or she is at fault. This can happen for a variety of reasons:

- the organisation has no considered policy on bullying, and the response is an instinctive attempt to avoid or deny the issue
- the complainant's version of events is disbelieved out-of-hand
- the bully lies, and his or her version of events is accepted without investigation
- the bullying is recognised, but the organisation is unwilling to deal with the bully
- the bullying is not recognised, because the bullying behaviour is considered to be acceptable within this particular organisation

Make an official complaint

Making an official complaint about bullying to an appropriate line manager or to the personnel department may halt a bully in his or her tracks. Sometimes, however, the complaint will be poorly dealt with, or the people to whom you make your complaint (and who represent the organisation you work for) will give their support to the bully rather than to you.

When making an official complaint:

- be sure of your actions, if you implement the formal grievance procedure;
- explain the situation clearly, without embarrassment;
- be sure your facts are right before you make any firm accusations;
- keep a record of events from the time you began to experience problems – refer to specific events, giving times and places and the names of any witnesses present;

> • remain calm. Remember that the company official to whom you complain formally could become a helpful source of support for you if he or she finds your case to be reasonable.

Ignore the bullying

On weighing up the possible options and their consequences, some people may choose to live with the bullying situation and act as if it is not happening. This might happen when the circumstances are expected to change soon, or when a recipient urgently wants to keep the job for some reason, such as:

- its importance in career terms
- its provision of pay, which is needed to live and/or to support dependants
- its level of pay, which is considered high enough to justify toleration of bullying

Be cautioned, however, that the bullying could worsen, and the eroding effects on your personality and behaviour are likely to be more harmful than you realise.

Find another job

Sometimes, the only realistic option open to a bullied person is to find another job, and to tolerate the bullying until he or she can move on.

Resign at once

If you do not want to challenge a situation of workplace bullying but find the bullying impossible to tolerate, your only option is to resign at once and seek other employment afterwards. However, this is a risky path to take because:

- there is no guarantee of finding equal work
- your resignation will have to be explained to future employers
- you may get no reference from the previous employer
- you will not be able to claim immediate financial help from the state

Having said that, many people, despite all of the above, do resign from positions where they experience bullying and go on to acquire another worthwhile job afterwards.

Take legal action

Legal action to challenge workplace bullying is a possible
way forward in some cases. The options here are limited,
and the process is likely to be costly and demanding, but
cases are sometimes fought successfully, especially when
illegal discrimination can be proven as a factor. The legal
options will be considered tomorrow.

You should be aware that a deliberate bully will want you
to be demoralised, and will depend on your not putting up
any resistance. Often, just standing up to the bully, while it
has its risks, will stop his or her aggressive activities.

Whatever you do, make sure that you talk to someone
about what is happening to you, so that you do not feel
that you are completely alone in this.

Summary

Today we have learned how to distinguish normal
behaviour problems from bullying, to handle conflict and
criticism, and to forestall such potential bullying. We have
then looked at the possible response options of those
bullied at work.

Tomorrow, we will go through some possible sources of
support and advice that you can turn to, and then look at
the legal situation with regard to workplace bullying.

Support for those bullied at work

There are various sources of support for people who are
bullied at work, and we will look at some of them today.
The legal context of workplace bullying and the various
options that could apply will then be explored.

Sources of support, information and advice

Even if you have decided to try to ignore bullying at work,
there are various support services and sources which you
should still seek out. Some possibilities are suggested
below.

Medical
Because of the effects over time on mind and body, it is
strongly advisable that you visit your doctor when you
know you are being bullied, and tell him or her about what
is happening in your working life. Your doctor may be able

to help you to some extent, by monitoring your state of mental and physical health, providing treatment if necessary, and warning you if things become bad enough to make absence or departure from work a medical necessity. In the event of any crisis or dispute connected with the bullying, the medical records could become important.

Trade unions or professional associations
If you belong to a trade union, speak to your workplace representative, or contact a local official to seek support and legal help. Trade unions and professional bodies often have advisers or legal departments which can provide information, advice and moral support.

Family
Your closest family have a right to know what is happening in your life, especially as the effects of bullying at work could change or depress you very much. Your partner or relatives can be an important potential source of support, if you give them the chance.

Friends
You will need as much moral support from those who surround you as you can get, so tell your closest friends about what is happening. They can help simply by listening to your problems and making you feel less isolated.

Colleagues
If you have any colleagues in whom you can really trust, talk to them about what you are experiencing. Colleagues in whom you confide may also have heard about, witnessed or even themselves experienced bullying by the

same person, and therefore be willing to support your complaint. But be aware of colleagues' possible fears of consequences and reluctance to become involved.

Personnel departments

If there is a personnel or human resource management department, you can discuss your problem with its staff. Many people mistrust personnel officers and personnel departments in a bullying situation and cases of personnel departments breaking confidentiality, rejecting bullying complaints out-of-hand, or being dishonest in their responses to complainants are not difficult to find. At the same time, however, many cases of bullying are dealt with successfully by personnel departments.

Case study: leaving may not end workplace bullying

Gillian left her NHS post in poor health, following her complaint to Personnel about bullying. The complaint was, she considered, dealt with badly, and the Personnel Officer supported the accused bully rather than Gillian.

After leaving, Gillian tried to get other NHS work on either a permanent or a temporary basis, but found it difficult, and had several experiences of sudden, negative changes of attitude from prospective or temporary employers. She eventually became convinced that she was being blacklisted in some way.

On one occasion, she knows her previous Personnel Officer contacted an office where Gillian had found temporary work. The day after that telephone call, Gillian was told her services were no longer required, although up to that point they had been well received.

You know your organisation better than anyone else, and if you feel it is possible to trust and make use of its personnel or human resources department, officials there often provide valuable support and advice for those who experience bullying at work.

Citizens Advice Bureaux

Volunteer advisers at your local CAB may be able to give you some idea of your legal situation and possibly give you access to their legal advisers, or to a volunteer who can help you through an employment tribunal.

Solicitors

Legal firms usually offer a free or low-cost initial advisory session, through which you can find out more about the legal options open in your case. Seek out a solicitor who specialises in employment law. Seek a second opinion if you are unsure about the advice you are given.

The Andrea Adams Trust

This Brighton-based Trust takes its name from Andrea Adams, broadcaster and journalist. Ms Adams, who died of cancer in 1995, did some ground-breaking reports for the BBC on workplace bullying during the 1990s. The Trust offers an information factsheet and support for people who are being bullied, and a consultancy service for organisations.

Workplace bullying – the legal context

Legal action on bullying at work should not be taken lightly. It will require finance, persistence and determination, as well as evidence, to pursue any form of action against either the bully or the organisation concerned. It should be remembered that legal processes work slowly, and you should always seek professional advice before deciding on any action.

There is, at present, no specific legislation relating to bullying at work in Britain. It can often be addressed indirectly through the legal system, though some of the possibilities given below remain, as yet, untried.

Legal provisions relating to bullying
Existing legal provisions could be drawn upon to fight a bullying case at law if the circumstances involve:

- constructive dismissal
- personal injury
- sexual, racial or disability harassment
- whistleblowing
- intentional harassment
- duty of care

Constructive dismissal

If circumstances force you to leave due to intolerable conditions, the situation could be construed as a constructive dismissal. Constructive dismissal occurs when an employee ends the employment contract (with or without giving notice) in circumstances where the employer's conduct has made continuation impossible.

Be warned, however, that:

- constructive dismissal is very difficult to prove
- it is necessary to give up the job to claim constructive dismissal
- you have to prove that continued employment was impossible for you

The implied contractual terms that are most frequently relevant to claims for constructive dismissal related to bullying are:

- *mutual trust and confidence:* when the employer's conduct destroys or damages mutual trust or confidence
- *reasonable support:* when the employer fails to take reasonable steps to ensure that the employee is supported in his or her duties without harassment or disruption from other employees
- *duty to provide a safe workplace:* when the employer fails to provide a safe working environment

There are time limits for unfair dismissal complaints, and any case should usually be presented at tribunal within three months of the date of termination. 'Out of time' claims may be accepted, but only if it can be shown that the applicant was not reasonably able to make the complaint within the time limit.

Personal injury

The Health and Safety at Work Regulations 1992 state that employers have a duty of care to assess risks to employees' health and safety, including their psychological well-being.

Actions should be taken to protect employees and prevent harm from identified risks. The duty of care covers mental as well as physical health.

Case study: a landmark case for employers' liability on stress

A landmark High Court case in 1995 awarded a Northumberland social worker £175,000 following a breakdown related to work stress. This case established a link between working conditions and mental ill health or stress. A psychiatrist attributed the social worker's breakdown to work pressure. On returning to work after his initial breakdown, the social worker did not receive the support his employers had promised. Following a second breakdown, he was dismissed on grounds of ill health. He sued his previous employers, and Northumberland County Council were found to be in breach of their duty of care.

Source: Bullying and Harassment at Work, IDS Brief, Employment Law Supplement 76, *May 1996*, p. 12.

Sexual, racial or disability harassment

Anti-discriminatory legislation in the form of the Sex Discrimination Act 1975, Race Relations Act 1976, and Disability Discrimination Act 1995 can be used to bring a case against bullying and harassment. This approach is currently used more than others by people who are bullied at work, but only applies if the recipient falls into a protected group. The case will rest on whether a person is treated less favourably on the ground of his or her sex, race or disability, and on whether the treatment led to dismissal, denial of opportunities or any other detriment.

Whistleblowing

Where people are bullied because they have blown the whistle on some practice or issue they consider to be wrongful and against the public interest, they may be able to make use of The Public Disclosure Act 1998 to fight their case.

'Whistleblowing' occurs when someone makes public events or practices which others want to keep secret. Whistleblowing by employees has in the past been a frequent cause of accusations of workplace bullying by the employing organisation, and is still likely to be relevant to some cases of bullying. But the Public Disclosure Act provides very strong protection against much workplace bullying that takes place within this context.

There is currently no compensation ceiling for whistleblowers who lose their jobs unfairly due to disclosure of corruption, fraud or worse.

The Queensland Whistleblower Study

This study identified levels and types of bullying behaviour reported by whistleblowers:

1 *Official.* Experienced by 71 per cent of respondents: deliberate, punitive responses veiled behind policy and procedure to avoid charges of illegality. These included selective redundancy, poor performance reviews, formal reprimands, punitive transfers, compulsory referrals to psychiatrists or other professionals, demotion, suspension, dismissal.

2 *Unofficial.* Experienced by 94 per cent of respondents, and frequencies higher: offensive but subtle, ambiguous or deniable workplace interactions. These included ostracism (experienced by all of the 94 per cent), spreading of rumours, questioned motives and personal attack, close scrutiny of work, abuse by colleagues, physical isolation, overwork, underwork.

Source: Bullying – From Backyard to Boardroom, *P. McCarthy, M. Sheehan and W. Wilkie, Alexandria, NSW, Millennium Books, 1996.*

Intentional harassment
The Criminal Justice and Public Order Act 1994 created a criminal offence of intentional harassment. An individual, whether at work or elsewhere, can be convicted for

intentionally harassing and causing alarm or distress to others. Criminal offences under this law might cover:

- threat
- verbal abuse
- insult
- violent assault
- persistent following
- the hiding of property
- damage to property
- harassing visible signs or displays

Harassment is defined as 'the use of threatening, abusive or insulting words or behaviour, or disorderly behaviour' in the Act. This includes the display of harassing signs or visible representations.

The Protection from Harassment Act 1997 (popularly known as the 'anti-stalking law') could also offer protection to employees who are bullied at work. The activities it covers include any persistent conduct (including words as well as action) which causes harassment or distress. The right to protection should apply anywhere, including the workplace.

The Dignity At Work Bill

A private Bill sponsored by the Manufacturing, Science and Finance (MSF) union was introduced to the UK Parliament in early 1997 that aimed to make it illegal for someone to deliberately bully another employee at work. The Dignity At Work Bill sought to establish a right to dignity at work, together with a right to take any bullying case to an employment tribunal.

The Bill failed to complete its passage through the House of Lords, due to the dissolution of Parliament in June 1997.

A similar Private Member's Bill, however, is proposed
for the future.

Duty of care – European law

Employers have a 'duty of care' under European law to
ensure the well-being of employees. But it could take five
years or more and cost a great deal of money to bring a
case through the European court.

Human rights law

The Human Rights Act 1998, in effect from the year 2000 in
Britain, will come into play where people consider that
their rights (as defined in the European Convention on
Human Rights 1951) have been denied. Once it is effected,
human rights cases which would have needed to go to the
European court can be heard in a British court. The Act
will state that individuals should not be subject to
degrading or inhuman treatment, and is likely to become a
weapon with which to fight bullying at work.

Summary

Today we have looked at some sources of support for
people bullied at work, and considered the legal options
available.

Tomorrow, we will consider ways in which organisations
themselves can support people who are bullied at work,
and deal with problem behaviour amongst employees.

Controlling bullying in the organisation

> But who is going to work well when they are both
> afraid and tired as a result of workplace bullying? It
> is amazing to me that any organisation is prepared to
> condone an atmosphere of infectious fear, simply
> through its inaction.
>
> *Lyn Witheridge, Chief Executive, Andrea Adams Trust*

Today we will consider the possibility that some people
might be more likely to experience bullying because of their
personality type, and think about why organisations need
to act to protect people from bullying.

We will then look at:

- protecting people who are bullied
- rebuilding recipients' confidence
- dealing with the bully

Vulnerability to bullying

It is sometimes claimed that there are individual
personality types who are more likely than others to
experience bullying and who unconsciously attract or seek
out situations in which they will be bullied.

Repetition compulsion

The psychoanalyst Leonard Shengold has argued that
child abuse in a 'totalitarian' household can lead to a
'repetition compulsion' in abused individuals. As
adults, he argues, these individuals will unconsciously
seek situations in which, either as the tormentor or as

the recipient, their experience can be repeated. This perspective creates a close link between bullying and being bullied in psychological terms.

Unfortunately, there is no workplace research to establish whether some people have internal conflicts that lead them to seek or contribute to situations of abuse. Certainly, it is generally recognised that low self-esteem and lack of confidence will make a person extremely vulnerable to bullying or manipulation. However, theories which suggest that some individuals are likely to attract bullying should not be used to move the responsibility for bullying onto the recipient.

Responsibility for bullying in a work context

Special factors apply to work which suggest a need to protect people from bullying. At work, people may have to tolerate or adjust to relationships which they would easily be able to escape outside work. To earn a living and keep a clean career record, we may sometimes have to:

- accept unfair management authority
- conform with a disagreeable workplace culture
- work with colleagues whom we find difficult

In the workplace, human relationships involve necessity, power and authority, and the employer who delegates authority needs to ensure it is exercised well.

Policy extract

QUESTIONING THOSE WHO COMPLAIN OF WORKPLACE BULLYING

To begin to understand the complaint and establish the facts, there are certain questions the manager will need to ask of the complainant, sensitively and tactfully using open questions to establish the circumstances, i.e.:

- What happened?
- Who was involved?
- Where did the incident take place?
- When did it occur?
- How did they react at the time?
- Were there any witnesses?
- Was this the first such incident or had something similar or the same thing happened before?

- Have they discussed the incident with any one else?
- Have they taken any action to stop further harassment?

Source: Management Guidelines on Harassment 1998
Oxfordshire Learning Disability NHS Trust

Dealing with unconscious bullying

If caught before a crisis is reached, a situation involving unconscious bullying can sometimes be resolved informally, where the bully is willing to:

- accept a critique of his or her behaviour
- try to change it
- let the situation be monitored for a period

Normal disciplinary procedures can be used if an intervention is made before too much damage is done.

If there is a trade union presence in the organisation, try to work with its representatives to deal with the situation. It is possible that both the bully and the recipient will be trade union members.

Why bullying should not be tolerated

It is gross misconduct

It usually involves the abuse of power by organisational agents

It creates health problems

It is demotivating

It causes absence

It causes people to leave

It is mismanagement

It destroys lives and personalities

Dealing with deliberate bullying

Cases of deliberate bullying do not usually come to light until a recipient – or, more likely, one person in a series of recipients – is desperate enough to make a complaint.

Case study: serial bullying

Gillian's complaints about bullying all failed to resolve the situation. People seemed sympathetic, but no action was taken, and she felt she was being batted back and forth between different people. The person she complained about was defended, and it was even suggested that Gillian was paranoic.

When Gillian pursued her complaint through use of the official grievance procedure, the attitudes of personnel and management staff became openly hostile. But she discovered that:

- the previous PA had walked out of her job, due to the behaviour of the bully
- another worker in the department had retired early and suffered a severe mental breakdown because of the bully
- the bully had a reputation for being difficult throughout the organisation

One of the other women who had experienced the bullying was prepared to give evidence to support Gillian's case, though the third recipient remained too ill to do so.

The serial bully was retired early as a result of the case, but for Gillian and the other two known recipients, it was too late. The damage was already done, their health had suffered permanent damage and their jobs were lost.

To fight the fear which usually prevents people from complaining about bullying until damage has already been done, an environment needs to be created within which complainants are protected from further bullying.

- Every organisation should ensure that there is someone outside reporting lines to whom bullied people can turn, and that this contact is well-communicated
- Every complaint must be taken seriously and investigated
- The complainant must be sure of confidentiality
- The bully should be removed from influence over, and interaction with, the complainant until investigations are completed
- If bullying is proven, the complainant should not have to work with the bully again
- Complainants should not be disciplined or penalised unless the complaint is found to be dishonest or malicious
- The organisation's lack of tolerance for bullying behaviours should be clearly communicated
- Preventative policies and complaints procedures should be known to all

The need for immediate support

Whenever people complain of being bullied at work, then immediate support and action from the employer is required. If the complainant is in any way at fault, this can be objectively evaluated during the process of dealing with workplace bullying.

If the bullying has reached a crisis stage, and the complainant is afraid and unable to work with or face the bully, remove the accused to prevent further interaction and even visual contact with the bullied person.

If the removal is found to be undeserved, redress should be made at a later stage.

Be aware that moving the bully to another department or activity could lead to further bullying problems in the department to which he or she is removed.

Managing bullying in small businesses

Preventing contact between disputing parties, if someone complains of bullying, is always difficult but is necessary to protect a complainant if he or she is distressed. For a small business it can be crippling. It is, therefore, particularly vital for small-business owners to prevent the development of bullying.

Stress is also a factor that may make bullying a particular problem in the small-business sector, because owners or managers are often under great pressure to keep the business operational and growing. Small businesses may sometimes lack:

- a full personnel function

- trade union representation
- any manager outside the line between owner and worker

These factors can all further contribute to the problem of bullying within small businesses.

In fact, in the case of bullying in very small businesses, it is most often the owner or manager who is complained about. Under current law, those who work directly for a small-business owner who is a bully and who is unwilling to discuss or change his or her behaviour, will find it difficult to fight without leaving the employing organisation.

Conciliation

If the bullying has not yet reached a stage where the recipient is unable to face the prospect of being with the bully, conciliation may be achieved, on the basis of the bully's ability and willingness to be honest about what has happened and to try to change.

A three-way meeting between the bully, the recipient and the facilitating company or trade union representative can:

- bring the recipient's complaint into the open
- let the bully know that his or her behaviour appears to be the problem
- advise that the aim of the meeting is to explore the possibility of the bully continuing in-post

The bully may be open to criticism and prepared to undertake training and to change his or her behaviour, while the recipient may be willing to return to the work relationship under controlled conditions.

Mediation

Mediation can be a very constructive possible approach, if the bully and the recipient are still willing to discuss the situation together.

The mediation process
Mediation is a structured way of dealing with disputes, using the mediation skills of one or two people who are impartial to the dispute, and trained in managing conflict. It has to be accepted voluntarily by all parties, and should be totally confidential. Mediators help participants to work through the situation of perceived or actual bullying. The aim is to change the situation through resolving communications problems and building a better relationship.

1   The mediator interviews the disputants separately to find out what is actually happening, what is perceived to be happening, and what each of the parties involved wishes to do about the situation.

2   If everyone concerned agrees that mediation is worth trying, the mediator sees the parties together and sets out the standards of polite, respectful behaviour which must operate if a successful outcome is to be reached.

3   Each party gives his or her version of the bullying that is alleged to have occurred. The mediator listens, and summarises what he or she has heard.

4   Possible misunderstandings and underlying issues are clarified by the mediator, who needs to be skilled in dealing with emotions involving anger and tearfulness.

5   Any causes of conflict that can be identified are discussed. The mediator tries to help each person to seek acceptable solutions.

6   An informal agreement to end the bullying or perceived bullying is reached verbally and written down by the mediator. Copies are given to and accepted by the disputing parties. It is then their responsibility to make the mediated arrangements work, possibly with the support of further mediation sessions, but without enforcement from the mediator.

If resolution proves impossible, the mediation process may at least help participants to make necessary decisions on their future courses of action.

Mediation can be introduced before a more formal grievance procedure is implemented, and, if it works well, is a recognised means of reducing the time, expense and stress of more formal channels and procedures.

Rebuilding confidence and morale

It will be necessary to rebuild the confidence and morale of the complainant, possibly by using means such as:

- *peer support groups:* colleagues of the recipient may have witnessed or experienced the bullying behaviour. They will benefit psychologically from seeing that their employer does not tolerate bad behaviour.

  The complainant, if able, may benefit from discussing the bullying experience with colleagues, in the context of facilitated, confidential and supportive work meetings.

  It is possible that some or all of the people in the recipient's work group were aware of the bullying but ignored it, or even gave it support through their alignment with the bully, or through allowing the bully to isolate the recipient.

  If so, this form of mutual group support may help them to come to terms with their own role, as well as encourage them to act differently if the same sort of circumstances occur again.

- *counselling support:* because of the potentially severe and long-term effects of bullying, immediate counselling support should be offered to the complainant, to help him or her to recover and begin to rebuild his or her life.

Counselling support may also be offered to the bully's spouse and family, who are likely to have been badly affected by the complainant's experience.

Dealing with the bully

There is no alternative to acting on complaints that are made about bullies, but this does not mean that the person or persons accused of bullying should be presumed guilty until proven innocent.

Dismissal of workplace bullies

A 1980 case (*British Home Stores Limited* v. *Burchell*) held that employers must establish a genuine belief, after full investigation, that a person's behaviour justifies dismissal. If this test is satisfied, dismissal will often be a reasonable way of responding to workplace bullying, especially if a warning has been given and disregarded.

Source: Bullying and Harassment at Work, IDS Brief, Employment Law Supplement 76, *May 1996, p. 15.*

The aim should be to protect and act with compassion towards all parties, including the accused bully or bullies. He, she or they must be moved out of contact with the recipient if the latter is distressed, but should not be treated as culpable unless guilt is proven.

Measures to deal with known bullies

Bullying behaviour cannot be tolerated, and must be penalised. For the sake of the recipient, continued employment of the bully may be out of the question. But sometimes, it may be possible and preferable to retain and retrain a bully.

Should the organisation consider that it does have some responsibility to offer the bully some support as well as discipline, measures to take might include:

- psychotherapy
- counselling
- group therapy
- close monitoring of future behaviour
- behavioural training

The bully should not gain from what has happened by being moved to a better job. This would be very demotivating for recipients or other staff.

A known bully should only be promoted when sufficient time has elapsed (at least two years) to show that he or she has succeeded in changing the bullying behaviour pattern.

Summary

Today we have considered whether some people are particularly vulnerable to bullying and looked at how people who are bullied at work can be protected and supported. We then explored how the bully can be dealt with.

Tomorrow, bullying will be looked at within the wider management context, and the role of formal policies to control bullying will be considered.

Bullying and management

Today we will look at:

- factors contributing to the increase in workplace bullying
- monitoring to detect the signs and symptoms of workplace bullying
- drawing the line between strong management and bullying
- key features of policies on workplace bullying

Bullying in context

Bullying is not a new problem, even though current research seems to suggest it is widespread. In 1971, working days lost through mental illness were extremely high, and bullying at work was recognised to be a major cause of this problem.

The vast increase in the reporting of workplace bullying over the past few years is partially due to:

- greater interest in workplace bullying
- increased public awareness of bullying
- increased awareness of the right to be treated with respect
- higher expectations concerning employment conditions
- campaigns to highlight workplace bullying

At the same time, however, people are under increasing pressure to:

- meet high targets
- do more with less
- work longer and harder
- take on more responsibility
- deal with change

These pressures, together with general job insecurity, rationalisation and company mergers, are known to have increased workplace stress and the likelihood of bullying.

Signs and symptoms of bullying at work

Where bullying is occurring, it is not usually clear to anyone outside the bullying relationships, but there are signs you can look out for that flag the risk of bullying in departments or work areas, and give warning of the need to investigate further.

Across the organisation, look out for departments or work areas where:

- people seem isolated

- productivity falls
- stress levels are high
- absenteeism is high
- staff turnover rates are high
- long-term sick leave occurs without clear physical reasons
- morale seems low

Monitoring for bullying

Related to the above, there are various indicators that can enable possible bullying to be picked up through personnel monitoring procedures. These include:

- statistical information showing high labour turnover, high sickness absence levels, lowered productivity or reduced work quality
- behavioural information, indicating lowered morale, increased apathy, loss of commitment, reduced creativity or heightened stress levels
- overworking: bullied people, ironically, may work longer hours than those who are not bullied, as part of their defensive reaction to the bullying problem.

If there are signs of a bullying problem, explore further by looking for possible changes such as:

- changed heads of department or supervisory personnel
- lowered performance from previously reliable employees
- new personnel
- higher numbers of dismissals, especially if recommended by a new boss

If the situation warrants it, check on the references and past records of anyone who the circumstances suggest may be bullying others.

Preventing and controlling workplace bullying

- Develop a policy to prohibit bullying
- Have procedures in place to deal with complaints of bullying
- Make sure the policy is publicised
- Monitor the policy and procedures to check their effectiveness
- Train people on the issues involved and on how to recognise bullying by themselves or by others
- Set up communication lines and support for those who may perceive themselves to be bullied
- Consider setting up a telephone helpline to monitor bullying, and support recipients

The need to draw a line between managing and bullying

It may sometimes be difficult to draw the line between the legitimate use of authority and the beginnings of bullying behaviour. People who have a strong management style and are working within a pressured environment may find themselves accused of bullying by some employees, even though they are unlikely to view themselves as bullies.

Case study: the 'can do' supervisor

Outside work, Mary was charming, but during working hours she was known:

- to be difficult and explosive with colleagues and subordinates
- to give her staff a hard time

- to set impossible work targets
- to exert a high degree of control over even the smallest things

Mary was often applauded for taking on and completing big workloads. But staff turnover and absenteeism within her department were high, and people who worked for her were often upset and stressed.

Four known complaints were made about Mary over 10 years, and her manager just warned her to try to change her behaviour.

If only one of the people who complained about Mary had successfully taken their case further, her behaviour probably would have cost her employers far more than it saved, even without the hidden costs of retraining, recruitment and demotivation.

Others, however, may know they are bullying others too much but consider that their behaviour is justified by the circumstances.

Setting standards of behaviour

Tolerating bullying, even in the interests of big cost savings, is irresponsible management because:

- more employees are now willing to challenge bullying behaviour, using existing legislation to exact possible high penalty costs
- public relations problems can be caused by people who bully others
- future legislation targeting workplace bullying is a growing possibility
- bullying is damaging to an organisation's culture

So how can an organisation draw the line between acceptable management behaviour and bullying? Perhaps a first tenet of management, after defining objectives and goals, should be defining exactly what is and is not reasonable in terms of the management behaviour through which objectives are to be pursued, and then establishing that standard of behaviour firmly, from the top down.

Extract

Harassment At Work Policy 1998

Oxfordshire Learning Disability NHS Trust

Purpose of policy

This policy sets out the standard of behaviour that the Trust expects of all its employees.

It – emphasises the need to treat everyone fairly

– draws attention to the many forms of harassment at work and to their serious adverse effects

– makes explicit those behaviours which the Trust will not tolerate, and

– provides practical guidance to all employees on how to deal with harassment, victimisation and bullying.

Managers have a responsibility for:

– ensuring that the policy is implemented

– communicating the policy to employees, and

– ensuring any complaints of harassment made against or by a member of their staff are treated seriously and dealt with appropriately.

But every Employee has a responsibility not to behave in a way that could be offensive to others nor to collude with others in doing so.

Policies and procedures to deal with bullying

In order to prevent bullying, its serious effects have to be recognised and accepted as damaging enough to require preventative action.

It is in an organisation's interests to:

- focus on what is and is not acceptable behaviour towards people within the business
- draw up guidance to clarify the line between rightful management and bullying
- draft a policy to prevent bullying

A perspective of sympathetic response to people who perceive themselves as bullied at work is a key aspect in creating a bully-proof working environment. Much else falls into place around that key response, including the need to be pro-active in detecting bullying before it becomes a crisis rather than a problem.

A well-staged policy to deal with bullying should act to prevent potential bullying from reaching a crisis point. It should also improve working relationships generally by taking a trouble-shooting approach to everyday conflicts, disagreements and performance problems.

Extract

Management Guidelines on Harassment 1998

Oxfordshire Learning Disability NHS Trust

Dealing with complaints of harassment, victimisation or bullying

Complaints may be received formally or informally from the complainant. All breaches of this Policy, however, must be treated seriously and Managers are responsible for ensuring that every complaint is dealt with promptly, correctly and with complete confidentiality. If the action taken is not effective and the breaches continue then Managers have a responsibility to take further appropriate action.

It is important, however, that any policies and procedures that are introduced are actually applied, that they are well-publicised, that relevant training is given on bullying, and that people are not afraid to use the procedures when necessary.

The words 'bully' and 'bullying' are recognised as being highly emotive, and some organisations may avoid their use in policies aimed at preventing bullying behaviour. Caledonian University, for example, developed a harassment policy which seeks to encourage, and give people the confidence to make, legitimate complaints. The University's policy includes extensive backing through the development of a network of trained volunteer harassment advisers. It also gives a guarantee of support and protection, unless the complaint proves to be mischievous or malicious.

Rather than bullying, however, the policy largely refers to 'personal harassment', as well as to sexual or racial harassment.

Extract

Harassment policy, staff & students 1997

Glasgow Caledonian University

Personal Harassment

Uninvited and unwanted behaviour by one person or group against others which may cause offence and/or embarrassment which creates fear, stress and tension.

Examples:
- improper, offensive and humiliating behaviour, practices or conduct, which may threaten a person's security (job/course)
- insensitivity to religious beliefs/persuasion
- constantly chipping away at a person's morale and their standing within a working team
- verbal or physical intimidation, ostracism or conversely excessive supervision.

Note
The events that lead to concerns/complaints of harassment may vary substantially, according to all the circumstances of the individuals involved. It is recognised that only the individual member of staff or student can determine what is offensive. It is therefore the **impact** of the conduct that is the determinant, not the **intent** of the perpetrator.

Writing policies on bullying

Ideally, organisations should focus on the possibility of bullying *before* complaints are received. Most, however, only consider policies and actions to prevent bullying after the damage has been done through inappropriate responses to a received complaint.

Littlewoods – Dignity At Work
Littlewoods was one of the first UK organisations to develop an in-depth anti-bullying policy and train people to act as supporters and investigators in situations involving bullying. The anti-bullying policy was introduced some years ago as part of the organisation's existing Dignity At Work policy. The

> policy has led to the resolution of many problems of bullying through informal rather than formal procedures, and has supported the effective functioning of the business.

A few organisations now have written policies to deal with and attempt to prevent bullying, and some research or trade union bodies have suggested policy guidelines. Organisations that were among the first to develop policies and guidelines to protect employees against workplace bullying include Littlewoods, British Telecom, the Consumer's Association, the Manufacturing, Science and Finance Union (MSF) and the Police Federation.

Corporate culture and workplace bullying

The climate within an organisation can encourage or discourage bullying behaviour, and in many organisations, permission to bully is given by default through ignoring the subject.

There are strong links between organisational culture and bullying, and sometimes bullying is an established and even implicitly approved approach to managing an organisation. The military and paramilitary contexts illustrate these links, in that they train to instil obedience by rank, and seek to prepare people for operational action. In this environment, behaviours that become bullying can evolve from efforts to build up a tough, like-minded grouping.

The initiation-type behaviours in some fire-fighting forces, for example, can involve a strong element of banter, pranks and physical jousting, and sometimes this fun has been known to go too far. In such cases, people who are 'different' in some way, and do not fit in easily, have occasionally been bullied and harassed to an unacceptable degree.

Bullying and culture in the armed forces

The twin factors of a strict hierarchical organisation and work involving the management of violence lends itself to bullying at work. It is not by chance that the majority of questions asked in the UK Parliament around bullying have concerned bullying in the armed services.

Source: Bullying at Work, *paper by Neil Crawford of the Tavistock Clinic, Staffordshire University Business School, Conference Proceedings, 1998.*

Such harassment is now illegal if it focuses on women, members of ethnic minority groups or disabled people, and some expensive cases have been brought against various police, armed-forces and fire-fighting organisations.

In consequence, throughout the uniformed sector, great efforts are now being made to set limits within which an acceptable level of boisterous team-building can be tolerated, while bullying is prohibited and penalised.

In organisations outside the military context, factors such as competitive pressures, over-high targets and job insecurity can operate to create a culture that harbours bullying. As people become stressed by work demands, are afraid for their jobs and feel under-valued by their employers, they are more likely to bully each other.

Audit for bullying

To find out whether bullying is a problem in your organisation, an audit can be carried out, using employees' confidential views as the main source of information.

1	Plan what you seek to achieve through the audit.
2	Decide whether internal or external people will carry out the audit.
3	Set time scales.
4	Select those who should be involved.
5	Clarify what is meant by bullying within your organisation.
6	Decide how you will explore people's experiences of bullying.

7   Prepare for some resistance, and identify its possible sources.
8   Agree on inputs needed to assess any existing problem.
9   Formulate questions to ask.
10 Estimate the time, materials and costs involved.
11 Identify existing factors or processes that discourage bullying and that can be built upon.
12 Decide on the approach or combination of approaches you will take, such as questionnaires, group discussions or one-to-one interviews.
13 Ensure that a confidential, anonymous basis is guaranteed, so that people trust you enough to give honest responses.

If bullying is found to be an extensive problem, a strongly led change programme will be needed to make bullying a recognised, wrongful and penalised behaviour throughout the organisation.

Preventative strategies

To develop a culture within which bullying is positively discouraged, written policies and implemented procedures are central, but supporting processes are also necessary, especially in terms of recruitment, communications, performance management and training.

Recruitment
The recruitment process can be adapted to try to prevent the selection of candidates who might bully.

- References should be followed up properly and pro-actively
- Interview questions can be included to explore candidates' preferred management styles and levels of interpersonal behaviour
- Job descriptions can be written to emphasise the need for caring attitudes and good interactive skills
- Psychometric tests might be used to try to identify potential bullying personalities

The aim is not to exclude all candidates who vary minutely from an ideal but to set and reinforce a requirement for reasonable standards of behaviour, and identify those who have bullied before.

Communications

The importance of good, open communications policies cannot be over-emphasised when it comes to preventing workplace bullying, which thrives on secrecy.

- Policies on bullying should be well publicised
- Attitude surveys might be used occasionally, with questions related to bullying included
- Managers should be expected to maintain good communications with those who report to them
- Exit interview questions can be included to test for possible experiences of bullying

Performance management

Performance appraisals or reviews can play an important part in underpinning the prevention of bullying in organisations.

- Styles of management or leadership, and standards of behaviour, should come into the performance review
- Objectives could be set that are related to maintaining or improving the required standards
- An element of upward appraisal might be used to pick up possible bullying tendencies, and give individuals the opportunity to recognise the need for change themselves, rather than through complaints or reprimands

Training

Skills that can help to reduce bullying behaviours in the workplace

- communication
- conflict resolution
- interpersonal skills
- leadership
- negotiation
- stress management
- team building

Source: McCarthy P, Sheehan M and Wilkie W, Managerial Styles and their Effects on Employees' Health and Wellbeing. In Organisations Undergoing Restructuring, a report for Worksafe Australia. *Brisbane, Griffith University, 1995.*

Preventative measures to develop an organisation in which bullying has no place begin with training:

- to encourage awareness of bullying as a possible problem

- to enable people to know how to respond to bullying when they encounter it
- to help managers to deal with complaints of bullying

The development of people's 'softer', interactive skills is also important. We all need to learn:

- to be aware of our own behaviour, particularly when under stress or going through organisational changes
- to assist others in coping with change or high pressure at work
- to deal with our own emotions and be aware of the feelings of others

TAKE A LOOK AT YOURSELF

Training in these skills will have the added advantage of developing an individual's self-esteem, confidence and assertiveness. This will help him or her to become less likely to accept or attract bullying behaviour, as well as less likely to inflict it on others.

Employee assistance programmes (EAPs)
Some organisations operate employee assistance programmes (EAPs). A full EAP can counter bullying, along with many other personnel problems. It usually includes stress care and counselling services, both of which are known to help in reducing bullying.

Summary

Today we have looked at why workplace bullying has increased and what are its signs and symptoms. The distinction between strong management and bullying has been considered together with key features of policies on workplace bullying.

Tomorrow, we will go over the aspects of workplace bullying that we have discussed throughout the week, and draw some conclusions about key aspects of preventing bullying.

Beating the workplace bullies

Over the week, we have hopefully discovered that bullying
at work is a problem that can be countered at the
individual level through open and assertive interpersonal
communication. Within organisations:

- good interpersonal and departmental
  communications can prevent bullying situations from
  developing
- written policies and standards of acceptable
  behaviour can be set up and implemented to
  manage workplace bullying
- recruitment, communications, performance
  management and training structures can all be
  adapted to support the prevention of bullying at
  work
- an employee assistance programme can provide
  support and help to bullied people

On Sunday, we looked at the meaning of workplace
bullying and began to appreciate why its growth in the
workplace is a serious problem for both individuals and
organisations. Bullying can present a highly destructive
threat to a person's livelihood as well as their personality,
and is based on the abuse of some form of power.

Types of bullying include physical as well as psychological
violence, and a distinction was drawn between unconscious
and deliberate bullying behaviours. The many forms that
bullying can take were explored together with the extent of
its growth as a workplace problem.

Overall, we saw that bullied people at work are in a 'no-win' situation in that, if they bring a case to fight bullying, they usually lose their job at the end of it all.

The costs and effects of workplace bullying, as we found on Monday, are severe for both the recipients and their organisations. Individuals can be destroyed, and for organisations the hidden price in terms of efficiency, demotivation, absenteeism and recruitment is high. If a case related to bullying is brought against the organisation, there are obvious monetary costs, together with probable damage to the organisation's reputation.

Bullying behaviour has many causes and takes many forms, but some common characteristics can be identified, such as:

- insecurity
- 'Jekyll and Hyde' character
- over control
- dislike of being wrong
- dishonesty

We came to understand that bullies can be from any background and any working level. While much bullying at work is seniority-based, it can also come from other directions, including colleagues, reportees and customers. In fact, as already mentioned, occasional bullying behaviour is a very human characteristic of which most people will now and then be guilty. Persistent bullying, however, is the real workplace problem, and can be carried out with unspoken organisational authority, as well as through individual intent.

Bullying is an ambiguous issue in that it is very related to subjective perceptions and to different perspectives on situations. Distinguishing whether or not you are being bullied is, therefore, a first step in dealing with workplace bullying. On Tuesday, we learnt how bullying situations can be largely prevented by dealing with normal working conflicts and criticisms in an effective, assertive way.

We have to be realistic and understand that people cannot always behave perfectly, especially when working conditions become stressful. At the same time, however, we all have the right to be treated with respect, and people who are insecure or lack confidence may find it difficult to know when they should assert themselves, and how to do so. We saw how the basic principles of assertive behaviour depend upon remaining controlled and not becoming aggressive, even when faced with abusive or angry responses.

ASSERTIVE   AGGRESSIVE

If you become certain that you are being bullied, and that the problem cannot be dealt with through usual channels of communication, there are some immediate steps to take:

- log the bullying incidents precisely
- seek other evidence or witness support
- collect any evidential documents
- seek moral support
- seek legal support, if you think it necessary
- find out whether your organisation has a policy on harassment or bullying

Then go through all the response options that are open to you, and decide on the one you think it best to take. We accepted that, in some working circumstances, there may be no other option for you than to seek another job.

On Wednesday, we went through some of the various sources of support and advice available to those who are bullied at work.

Legal action to fight workplace bullying is no easy route to take, and there is no specific legislation to prevent bullying at present. But there are some ways of addressing the issue indirectly, particularly if discriminatory harassment can be proven on grounds of race, sex or disability. Existing legal provisions include constructive dismissal, which is likely to be the most relevant option in the UK, after discrimination. This, however, can be hard to prove and involves giving up your job in order to make the claim.

It is possible that some people are more prone to be bullied than others, as we saw on Thursday. People who are insecure and lacking in confidence may allow themselves to be bullied where others would resist, while people who have been bullied as children may unconsciously seek to repeat that situation as adults, either as perpetrators or as recipients.

Workplace bullying, however, is indiscriminate, and in many cases involves strong and confident individuals. Sometimes, those who relate experiences of workplace bullying consider that the person who bullied them was in some way resentful or envious of their success, ability or popularity, and possibly even found them to be a career threat.

Whatever the circumstances, bullying at work is in a special category which involves relationships of power and necessity. For this reason, as well as for reasons of professional management, organisations need to ensure that:

- delegated responsibility is exercised with responsibility and care
- policies to prevent and manage bullying are in place and adhered to

Because the effects of bullying on individuals are so severe, responses to complaints about workplace bullying have to be dealt with immediately and taken very seriously. Priority should be given to supporting the complainant unless and until conclusive investigations show the bullying claim to be invalid.

The bully may have to be either moved or suspended. This could be a big problem, especially for small and struggling businesses. At the same time, however, bullying should be more visible and manageable within a small business.

Good communications and procedures are central to the prevention, detection and control of bullying behaviour within organisations. In some complaints cases, reconciliation and mediation procedures may help all parties to find a means of resolving their problems, or at least to decide on a course of action.

MSF guidance on bullying policies

- Clearly define bullying and the forms it takes
- State that bullying will not be tolerated
- State that bullying will be treated as a disciplinary offence
- Guarantee confidentiality
- Work with trade union representatives

The policy should include a commitment to assess the risks of bullying and to correct deficiencies in the organisation that could cause or encourage bullying.

Recommended two-stage complaints procedure

1. *Informal.* Giving employees an opportunity to discuss the complaint with a trained volunteer who can listen, advise and help to resolve the problem.

2. *Formal.* Stating:

    - whether the bully will be suspended

    - how investigations will be made

    - the time scales for investigation

    - the complainant's right to representation

    - the appeal procedure

- the confidentiality requirement
- the availability of mediation
- disciplinary sanctions against bullying.

Review:

Make provisions for regular, joint monitoring and review of the policy, possibly including attitude surveys and/or exit interviews.

Additional provisions

- Publicising of the policy
- A network of trained counsellors
- Appropriate training about bullying and the skills needed to deal with it, for the workforce and for those implementing the policy
- Independent professional counselling for the bullied and for the bullies

Source: Bullying at Work: How to Tackle It,
MSF, London, 1995.

A bullying complainant is likely to be very demoralised, and possible approaches to giving him or her some support within the organisation include involving colleagues in discussing the experience, and providing professional counselling or psychotherapy.

Accused bullies should also be treated with care, and should not be assumed to be guilty unless and until the case is proven.

Where guilt is concluded, dismissal on grounds of misconduct is possible, and bullies should certainly be penalised. But some organisations may feel it worthwhile to try to rehabilitate, retain and support the bully if he or she agrees to appropriate training, counselling or monitoring measures.

A trouble-shooting approach to bullying that seeks to prevent and detect it before crises can develop is the key to its management within organisations. On Friday, it was suggested that bullying is linked to work pressures in organisations and the general context of growing job insecurity.

There are ways to detect bullying risks within an organisation, and to identify people who are possibly being bullied. Policies and procedures can be developed to prevent and control workplace bullying. But sometimes individuals will bully others without realising it, because they are intent on achieving high performance targets.

For this reason, there is a need to distinguish between legitimate and bullying managerial behaviour, setting firm standards of behaviour that are established from the top down and backing these with policies and procedures to detect and prevent bullying.

Written policies alone are not enough, however. They have to be implemented, and people have to be confident enough to use them.

Case study: a policy without substance

A contracts manager with a London borough sought to make use of its Harassment Policy. He reported many bullying incidents, including one during which he was sprayed with air freshener. He asked to use the counselling scheme via his line manager. The latter brought in the HR manager, and the complainant was asked to see an occupational health doctor for a 'capability test'.

When he later checked his personnel file, he found no reference to the bullying complaint, though the doctor's report was there. The complainant considers that the borough did not adhere to its own policy at all, and he has now resigned his post.

Rather than making people over-aware of workplace bullying, a positive approach to a written policy on bullying can emphasise the stringent requirement to always treat others politely and with respect.

CONFIDENCE   SELF-ESTEEM

Lastly, on Friday, the links between corporate culture or management styles and bullying were explored. Reference was made to culture in some uniformed services, and we looked briefly at possible preventative strategies using recruitment, communication, performance management and training. Employee assistance programmes were also mentioned.

Case study: how to teach people to bully

A recently arrived petty officer instructor was questioned by an officer about why he failed to shout at a cadet when addressing him. The petty officer answered that he saw no reason to shout, because the cadet did what was required of him when addressed in a normal voice.

The petty officer later commented that he can now see why so many junior officers arrive on board ship with an attitude problem about enforcing discipline below decks. They are taught to bully the ship's company rather than lead by example.

Summary and conclusion

Today, we have looked back over the ground we covered on workplace bullying during this week.

Overall, the best way to prevent bullying is to acknowledge it as a potential problem, with high penalties for both individuals and organisations, and develop a set of core values emphasising:

- respect for individuals
- good organisational communications at every level
- established standards of behaviour
- skilled interpersonal communications

OXFORDSHIRE LEARNING DISABILITY NHS TRUST

Important Information for all staff:

Harassment

Bullying

Intimidation

• are unacceptable

• are everyone's responsibility

• are not to be suffered alone

**If YOU are feeling harassed, bullied
or intimidated (or you feel someone else is)**
then please contact the following
for support/advice/someone to talk to
in the strictest confidence.

Please contact either:

- Human Resources Department
- Your Staff Representative
- Your Line Manager/Supervisor
- Occupational Health Dept

Source: Oxfordshire Learning Disability NHS Trust, 1998

Good behavioural standards are the best foundation for an
organisation which aims to banish bullying. For
individuals, too, high behavioural standards will help to
prevent bullying, and ensure that we treat others with the
respect that is their right.